The Book Of Miracles:

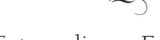

Extraordinary Experiences of Ordinary People

Written and Edited by
Sharron Davies

Copyright 1998 by Sharron Davies
All rights reserved.

**Publisher's Cataloging-in-Publications
(Provided by Quality Books, Inc.)**

Davies, Sharron (Sharron Lyniere)
 The book of miracles : extraordinary experiences of
ordinary people / written and edited by Sharron Davies.
 p. cm.
 ISBN 0-9722077-7-5

 1. Miracles. 2. Christian life. I.Title

BT97.3.D38 2003   231.7'3
                          QB103-700684

Printed by Bethany Press – United States of America

Dedication

This book is dedicated to my families of birth and new birth; to the Davies and Pryde families and the family of Believers.

Thank you for your love, guidance, teachings, support and prayers.

The Book of Miracles:
Extraordinary Experiences of Ordinary People

Acknowledgments

Section I: Miracles of Compassion 13
1. Thy Will Be Done
2. Let's Go Crazy
3. There is a River
4. The Bible

Section II: Miracles to Confirm Faith 33
5. Angela Imani - Joseph Montrel
6. An Issue of Blood
7. The Job
8. To Crack and Back

Section III: Miracles to Demonstrate Jesus as Lord and Savior 53
9. In God's Hand's
10. The Miracle of Threes
11. Monkey
12. ... But Now I See

Section IV: Miracles to Advance the Gospel 71
13. Signs and Wonders
14. Calming the Storm
15. Three Sisters
16. Divine Whisperings

Section V: Miracles to Deliver God's People 93
    17.   A Station Wagon Revival
    18.   The Investigation
    19.   The Next Time
    20.   Deadly Choices
    21.   Answered Prayer

Acknowledgments

Father God, for your infallible plan of Salvation; Jesus, for your exemplary sacrifice; Holy Spirit, for inspiration to begin, and nudging to complete, this work. To my husband, best friend and ministry partner, Martin, for your love, your great confidence in my ability to see this through, and belief in God's desire to use this book for His Divine Purpose.

Special thanks and blessings to all those who were willing to share intimate pieces of their hearts and lives through your stories, that the Kingdom of God should be enlarged.

Joan, confidante, spiritual navigator and road trip partner; to Pastor Lee and the Loudon Avenue Christian Church family, for spiritual growth and opportunities for deeper relationship with the Lord.

And to every heart and spirit that has touched mine in a miraculous way – I thank you.

Preface

The anatomy of a miracle is elusive and incomprehensible. If we look closely at the scriptures there are miracles that span many breadths, lives and witnesses. The anatomy depends on the situation, though the purpose remains the same – to show the reality, the power, and the intimate concern of God for the restoration of His people to Himself.

The Father wants us to BELIEVE on His Son Jesus as the true and only Messiah, that we may come to an intimate fellowship with Him through His Son. The echoing refrain from every miracle is: "this is the power and the *messenger* of God", or as the Farther so aptly said "this is my Son in who I am well pleased, hear ye him."

In John chapter two and verse eleven (John 2:11), Christ performs his first miracle at the wedding in Cana. "This miraculous sign at Cana in Galilee was Jesus' first display of his glory. *And his disciples believed in him*" (New Living Translation). Likewise, encouraging belief in the messenger and so therefore the message is again seen in verse 23 (John 2:23): "Now when he was in Jerusalem at the Passover, in the feast day, *many believed in his name, when they saw the miracles which he did.*" (King James Version) In John chapter seven, verse 31 (John 7:31), belief that Jesus was the Christ, the promised Messiah, is confirmed in the hearts of the people by the wonders he performed. *"And many of the people believed on him* and said, when Christ cometh, will he do more miracles than these which this man hath done?" (King James Version)

The Father approved the message of the Christ through miraculous signs made available to His people. As the message of Christ continues, so also do the miraculous demonstrations of God's Sovereignty. In the earthy life of Christ, the greatest miracles, those of the embodiment of God in Jesus, his resurrection, appearances and ascension, were critical to restoration of the relationship God desired with man; the very same one He designed in Eden at the beginning of mankind's time. It is that relationship He desires to maintain through eternity with all those who believe the message of the Gospel is true.

Miraculous signs follow messengers of every generation who are charged to carry the Gospel of Jesus Christ. Take note of the miraculous accomplished by the power of God through Philip in Acts 8:13 and Paul in Acts 19:11. This power was given them for the express purpose of confirming the message of salvation they carried.

The miraculous today is no different than that of the time of Christ and the Apostles. God's Power and Purpose – restoration of our original relationship with Him – have not changed; God continues to reveal glimpses of his Power and His desire to provide for our escape from eternal separation, through the miraculous. There is however, an open door of choice we each are given opportunity to walk through or to ignore. It is the door of acceptance of Jesus and a restored relationship with the Father – salvation.

This body of work is an assembly of miraculous stories as defined and relayed by those who experienced them. In this body, you will find many voices, yet one refrain: belief in the Christ and the Power of God's might. It is our prayer that you will also find a miracle in your own life.

> "How shall we escape, if we neglect so great salvation; which at the first began to be spoken by the Lord, and was confirmed unto us by them that heard him; God also bearing them witness, both with signs and wonders, and with divers miracles, and gifts of the Holy Ghost, according to his own will?"
>
> (Hebrews 2:3-4)

Section I:

~ Miracles ~
of Compassion

15 Miracles of Compassion

> "Where, O death, is your victory?
> Where, O death, is your sting?"
>
> - I Corinthians 15:55

A fact of our human existence is that we are creatures needing compassion in times of distress. We seek it from our families, from our co-workers, from our children, and from our neighbors in the world.

At no other time in the human experience is greater hurt and suffering felt than at the death of a loved one. It is during this time of sadness and loss that we most need a word of comfort, a soothing hand and a strong faith. Because death is the final enemy, the final place where Satan can try to control us, Jesus, in his compassion, is also there. He alone can take the sting out of death for believers. This power was shown through the miracles of resurrection performed in the New Testament and it is still shown today. In this section we will visit present day miracles of God's compassion within the human experience of death.

Contemporary dictionaries refer to compassion as "The deep feeling of sharing the suffering of another in the inclination to give aid or support, or show mercy."[1] Biblically, compassion has many definitions, for there are at least five Hebrew and eight Greek terms for compassion. One of these is *Oiktiro*, a word meaning lamentation and grief for the dead and which later came to mean sympathetic participation in grief. Such sympathy or compassion stands ready to help the one who has suffered loss.[2] Jesus showed such compassion in his roles as shepherd and high priest.

---

[1] The American Heritage Dictionary
[2] Holman Bible Dictionary

In Matthew, Mark, and John, Jesus compares his nature to that of a Good Shepherd, who constantly watches and protects his flock. Unlike the "hired hands" in John's gospel who cared nothing for the sheep, He promises not to leave us when wolves and other enemies attack and try to scatter us (John 10:11-12).

Jesus is our High Priest and mediator. In Hebrews, the Apostle Paul describes Jesus as the High Priest who is able "to sympathize with our weaknesses" (Hebrews 4:15). As our High Priest, Jesus sacrificed his life for us and through the resurrection overcame the last enemy: Death. He moved death from the end of our existence to the middle and promised us that after this earthly life, and after earthly death, we will live again eternally if we believe in Him. Therefore, we have no reason to fear or revere death. Yes, Death is an enemy - a defeated enemy (Hebrews 2:14-15).

Despite this knowledge, when death strikes many of us are like the crowds described in Matthew, "harassed and helpless" in our grief (Matthew 9:36). We have been taught by society that death is something to be feared and that it is the final chapter of our lives. Now as then, Jesus remains the Good Shepherd who has compassion, who knows us, and who is steadfast in his individual care for us. He is *still* the High Priest who understands, and who pleads our case before God, when we ask him to and often when we don't. He shares in our sorrows and stands ready to comfort us. It is this kind of personal concern for our welfare that Christ has always brought to His relationships with us.

We see this as we study the miracles of resurrection Christ performed. In Luke 7:12-15, we see Him raise from death the only son of a widow because "his heart went out to her." Without a husband or children, her life would be difficult. His compassion moved Him to act and return her son to life and to her. A second example is found in the Gospel of John at the death of Lazarus. Jesus is *"deeply moved in spirit and troubled"* at Mary's response to the death of her brother Lazarus. Again He stepped in to help by returning Lazarus to life (John 11:38-45) and to his sister. In Mark 5:35-42, the dead daughter of Jairus, a synagogue ruler, was brought back to life because her father "pleaded earnestly" with Jesus to restore her.

The performance of miracles today to show the Lord's power over death is no less striking, nor simplistic, than the miracles of the New Testament. The miracles that follow are testaments to the unchanging nature and power of God. Today he continues to demonstrate his compassion for us and his power over death.

Being able to rejoice and find comfort, solace and acceptance in the death of a loved one is very difficult. Through God's grace and mercy, and through His miracles in revealing the true nature of death to us, we are free to go on and live a life that is pleasing to Him unafraid.

As you step into the next pages, witness God's compassionate offer of life everlasting for all those who believe in Him and in His power over the final enemy - Death.

> *"Peace I leave with you; my peace I give you.*
> *I do not give to you as the world gives. Do not let your hearts be troubled and do not be afraid"*
>
> *- John 14:27*

Thy Will Be Done

My daughter Lauren's life, plagued by a chronic incurable illness, was an eerie panorama of peaks and valleys punctuated by plateaus that lowered after each medical crisis.

In November 1980, I sat with my husband and parents in an Intensive Care Unit waiting room anxiously awaiting the latest prognosis for Lauren, who at 24 had suffered her fifth massive hemorrhage. Seeing my deep concern, my Dad held my hands and said, "Let's pray the Lord's Prayer." Afterwards he said, "Lady, it's time; time to let her go. Give her up." I looked at him in disbelief as he continued, "We prayed Thy will be done. Didn't you mean it?"

I confessed to myself that it was just a rote prayer; left for the silence of the lounge and there prayed openly, remembering those words in Mark telling us to ask for our desires, believing and expecting the answer. My prayer was that Lauren would be restored and that we would both have the strength and the wisdom to endure. She was dearly loved and I could not conceive being separated from her, though it was inevitable. God answered that prayer in the affirmative but the long, difficult, recovery was emotionally and physically draining and had a tremendous impact on all of us. Was my prayer selfish? Had I unjustly sentenced both of us to lives of added pain: she imprisoned by a deteriorating existence, and me shackled not only to her, but to my own endless guilt?

The New Year 1993 found me trying fiercely to juggle several very stressful family situations. Only by the grace of God were all the balls kept in the air. Dad, while hospitalized for a broken jaw, suffered a heart attack and debilitating stroke. Mom, 91, frail, and very dependent, was at home alone. Lauren, weakened by a coronary and seizures, was also suffering from progressive kidney and liver failure. Life was like a frightening, never-ending ride on a roller coaster, with my guilt choking me at every turn. By early February, Dad's condition worsened. The Lord sent me to the emergency room with Lauren that night, and then led me to Dad's room.

I prayed as he breathed heavily, told him I loved him, hugged him and said my last good-bye. At 2 a.m he died peacefully. I felt so empty and alone, but there was no time to mourn and no shoulder to lean on. My mother was devastated. We found out Lauren had suffered another coronary, and the family was trying to deal not only with that emergency, but also with their own grief. I was moving, functioning through a sort of transience - anxious, agonized and restless within, but amazingly productive and calm on the outside. Exhaustion alone brought welcomed and needed sleep.

Early the morning of February 14th, I was awakened by a voice I immediately recognized as Dad's. He spoke calmly, "Lady, it's time; it's time to give her up. To say Thy will be done and mean it." It was again that November day 13 years ago. I didn't respond nor ponder over the message. I listened and then just drifted off into the most peaceful sleep I had known in months.

When I awakened, I felt refreshed, relaxed and warm, as if someone were embracing me. My customary morning prayer began and the words were unrestrained. When the prayer turned to Lauren, these were my words, "Thy will be done, O God." It was said with sincerity and expectancy and I knew I was ready to accept His answer.

A week later, we were preparing to take Lauren to dialysis. She ate her favorite pancakes and became ill, yet smiled and said those infamous words, "I love you, Mommie." She started having chest pains. I comforted her as my husband drove to the Dialysis Center. She hugged me and quietly slipped away in the car. That same peace just seemed to engulf me and sustained me as we watched the paramedics vainly try to revive her. They kept telling me "We can bring her back! We can bring her back!" But I thought, 'Back to what?' Oh, the loss was felt, but there was no searing pain or sorrow and no regrets. The staff moved her to the back of the room, sat her in a chair and pulled the privacy curtain around her. She looked so peaceful. As I sat with her body, awaiting the mortician, a song kept going through my mind, but later I could not remember what it was.

The family was home for the second funeral in three weeks. That first night, I was awakened by a figure in the darkened upstairs hallway, enveloped in the brightest (almost blinding) white, flowing robe I had ever seen. Unable to move or turn away, I watched as it went from room to room. When it turned, I knew it was my Lauren, hair swinging on her shoulders and her delicate little hands upraised. The idea came to me that she just wanted to see everybody; I just wanted to catch her, to touch her. I ran toward her as she started down the stairs. She no longer limped. She literally flew down both flights of stairs to the family room, running freely and then vanished. I returned to bed and as I lay down the song form the waiting room came back to me, like someone singing in my mind. This time I knew it.

"I'm free, praise the Lord, I'm free. No longer bound, no more chains holding me. My soul is resting; it's such a blessing. Praise the Lord, Hallelujah I'm free!" We were both free. She was free from a body wearied by disease, and I from the self-imposed and unwarranted guilt, which had tormented me for so long.

I thank God that the separation I had so feared had brought us both an abiding peace.

The story that follows is another incident related to Lauren's death as told by her sister.

> "Blessed are those who mourn,
> for they will be comforted."
>
> - Matthew 5:4

Let's Go Crazy

It had been a difficult year. My sister Lauren had been quite ill since early winter and had become more and more impaired. Every weekend the rescue squad, sirens and lights careening, would be summoned to resuscitate her. It was senseless to me.

Twenty-eight years had passed since Lauren had been diagnosed with Sickle Cell Anemia at the age of eight and she had since fought many battles with the disease. In the fall of 1992, she had been stricken with kidney failure and had begun dialysis treatments at noon on Mondays, Wednesdays and Fridays.

Christmas had been very hard, because Lauren was slipping away and though we did not know it then, it would be her last Christmas with us in the flesh. Amazingly, her wit remained, as did her sense of family responsibility. She always thought of others first; especially me. She always questioned my ability, as the 'baby', to make it in the world even though I lived alone in another city. It was torturous to watch her suffer, to watch her grow thin and weak. It was horrible to watch her not be able to stomach food, and then to stop eating. I prayed secretly that she would be released from the anguish in which she lived; and me from mine. It was just a matter of time - cruel time. I waited to hear the news and hoped that the day would not come.

Life and work ground on. It was February 22, 1993. A coworker and I decided on lunch downtown; I glanced at the clock as we headed out the door - 12:15 p.m. As we neared the downtown area, about fifteen minutes away, I was overcome by a strange burst of energy, a tremendously ecstatic feeling, and a vision of the heavens opening up to reveal an intense white Light swirling with a rainbow of color. Green light was the music that danced about the Light and there was a great and joyful "noise" of lights coming from inside the cloud. Then I heard a short lyric from the Prince song "Let's Go Crazy." I sang it out loud, "...*we're all excited. Don't know why. Maybe it's because, we're all gonna die.*" [3] The feeling and the vision disappeared nearly as quickly as they came. My companion asked if I was okay. I myself wondered where that feeling and that song had come from. It wasn't that it was so unusual for me to sing Prince's songs, since he had been my favorite artist for years. Though I had stopped listening to most of his music, when I did listen, I sang the songs all the way through. This was different. The song had come from nowhere. It was strange to burst in and out of song so passionately and so swiftly. I didn't try to figure it out.

That night I got the call from my parents. It was the news I had dreaded and prayed for. Lauren had died in the car that day on the way to her dialysis treatment. She had experienced cardiac arrest and my parents had tried to reach the Dialysis Center in time to prolong her life again. Rescue squad workers tried to resuscitate her once and failed. My parents wisely refused to continue the resuscitation effort and let Lauren go. Still, I was devastated, too shocked to cry and bordering on guilt for my Christmas prayers. How could someone actually pray for her sister to die?

---
[3] ©1984 Controversy Music ASCAP

Now it had come true. God had answered with a yes. My mind went whirling in twenty directions, from loss to limbo, to grief to guilt. I sat silently on the phone - everywhere and nowhere. Then, that strange moment at lunchtime flashed in my mind.

"What time did she die?" I asked.

"About 12:20 but they resuscitated her. She failed again at 12:25 and we let her go."

She had done it again. Before leaving for her new home, Lauren thought of me once again and had conspired with God to speak to me in a way they both were certain I would hear and remember. She wanted me to know that she finally was free, that my prayer had been answered in a way that was "exceeding abundantly more than I could ask or think". God wanted me to taste His sweetness, glimpse His glory and be at peace with my prayer. How amazing He is.

In that moment her spirit had merged with mine so that I could be one with her, and know, and taste and glimpse the very Spirit and Throne of God. And I was assured that the awesome ecstasy I felt for that moment was hers forever with Him.

> "In my Father's house are many mansions: if it were not so, I would have told you. I go to prepare a place for you."
>
> *- John 14:2*

There is a River

Growing up, I had a very close relationship with my father. He died accidentally when I was young, about 13. He had a boat and he and his best friend, Leonard, used to go fishing all the time. This time, Leonard's eight-year-old son went on the trip. While they were out that day, the boat stalled. A passerby asked if they needed to be towed in and tied the two boats together. It turned out the man who offered to tow them was drunk. He sped off too fast and the little boy was thrown off the boat; my daddy jumped in to save him and they both drowned. So I never got to say good-bye to him.

I still dream about my Dad and sometimes see him just as clearly as if he was alive, in my dreams. The last time I had a dream about him, I remember saying "Daddy, where are we?" because there were huge houses, like mansions - just huge houses. And he said "Well Shay, where do you think we are? Look at that river right there." There was a river coming down by the mansion and I said "What river is that, Daddy?" and he said, "That's the river Jordan." It was the weirdest dream.

One of the things I always worried about was if my daddy was saved. He hardly ever went to church; he would rather go hunting than go to church. The dream made me believe he made it to Heaven and that I will see him again there. I really feel that the spirits of our loved ones are around us and that they are watching over us. Every year around the time of my dad's death, I dream about him and it always has a calming effect on me. God promises us everlasting life and I believe in that promise.

> "*Ask and it will be given to you; seek and you will find; knock and the door will be opened to you.*"
>
> - Matthew 7:7

The Bible

My brother Charles and I were very close even though we were born nine years apart. He knew how to push my buttons, but that never mattered. We always knew we had that love between us and we were always there for each other. He was the first person I called when something happened and he was the godfather to both my children. Charles, a security guard at the Library of Congress, was always the type to deal with the here and now. If there were something he wanted, he would go out and get it. But he had been working so hard to get those things that he wasn't enjoying his life. At the age of 38, his perspective changed.

That year a position above his at work became available. It was also around that time that he began to have shortness of breath, but nothing else major. He was up for the promotion, so when the pain started, he didn't want to go to a doctor. He was worried about not getting a clean bill of health and then not getting the job. I kept telling him he should worry more about his health than about his promotion. He finally let me take him to the doctor, but they didn't know what was wrong.

A lot was happening at that time. There were the funerals. I think they may have been one of the things that opened his eyes. His Sergeant at work, who was a young man like Charles, died suddenly and several friends of his also died. When you see that you are not invincible and will not be around forever, you think about your life. He started going to church with his wife, a Seventh Day Adventist. He also went to many of those funerals, including his Sergeant's.

At the end of the service, the minister opened the doors of the church for anyone who wanted to accept Jesus Christ into their lives. Charles stood and soon a lot of other people followed and accepted Christ. I remember him telling that story and saying he wasn't sure what accepting Christ was really about, but as he stood there, tears started streaming down his face.

About a month after that, Christmas 1992, we were having dinner at my in-laws' house when the phone rang. My husband answered it and called me to the back of the house.

"Charles has died."

Earlier that day, at about 2 o'clock, we were at the house just sitting around and I experienced a severe chest pain. It was so strong that I had to sit down. When I asked my sister-in-law what time Charles died, it was just about the same time that I had experienced that pain. I believe that was his way of alerting me, so I would know when he had gone on.

She told me he had been at home relaxing when he started having chest pains again. This time, they were so severe he slumped out of his chair. She had called the rescue squad, but they were unable to save him. He died in the hospital shortly after he arrived.

Strangely enough, the week before Christmas, my whole family had been home and so we had an early Christmas dinner and celebration. It was unusual because we were not normally all in the same city. God gave us a chance to celebrate Christmas all together before Charles' death. Even more strangely, when we pulled out of my parents' driveway that night, I remember having the distinct feeling that we would never all be together again.

After the funeral, I stayed with my sister-in-law in Maryland for a week to help out. We were talking about Charles and how he had been seeking answers. He had been going to church and talking to the pastor. As we talked, she asked me a religious question. We needed a Bible, so she brought his out to look for the answer. For some Reason, I felt compelled to ask her if I could have his Bible. She said yes and gave it to me.

When I got back home I was looking through the Bible and I saw that Charles had highlighted different passages and scriptures about salvation - that led me to believe he knew his time was coming and he had been looking for answers. In finding Christ, he had found the answers. That set me at ease and let me know he was okay.

It was a very eye opening experience for me, especially the peace that I felt throughout that entire time. Even though his death was unexpected and on Christmas Day, there was a definite peace that swept over me. That made it easier for me to cope with his death and to help other members of the family cope with it, too.

Through the highlighted passages in his Bible I knew he was all right. One passage was "Who will be saved?" I had comfort knowing that Charles had been. He had found the Savior, Jesus Christ, and he would be all right moving from this life to the next.

When you know that you are a child of the Most High God, you can get through anything regardless how difficult the situation may be, knowing you have come through the Valley of the Shadow of death. There is nothing else that quite compares to that; if you have been there and come back out in peace, you know by the grace of God you can survive and find peace in anything.

Section II:

Miracles to Confirm Faith

Miracles to Confirm Faith

> *"Now faith is the substance of things hoped for,*
> *the evidence of things not seen."*
>
> -Hebrews 11:1

Imagine yourself in a courtroom. You are the sole jurist, seated alone in the jury box, awaiting the opening arguments of an important case. Seated before you to the left are the defendant and his lawyer, a well-respected woman and close friend of yours; the prosecuting attorney; and an audience of observers. To your right is the judge. There is a call to order in the courtroom and the docket is read. The defending attorney now rises to address you.

"Your Honor and Jury member. The man seated before you has been charged with a serious crime. I know that he is innocent. My charge over the next week is to convince you of his innocence. This is a highly unusual case. You see, I have no evidence to support my argument. There are no defense witnesses and no other suspects. The prosecution has what looks like evidence, but it is false evidence, which *appears* to be real. It looks real, feels real and sounds real. It is not.

"This man IS innocent. Though I cannot prove that through the normal courtroom procedures, it is true. I believe it and I ask you to believe also. I ask you to believe, not based on what you will see. Not based on what you will feel. Not based on what you will hear. I ask you to believe because you know me. I do not lie and I would not lead you astray. My plea with you is to find this man not guilty; not because of anything that you know about him, but because of everything you know about me."

Certainly, this kind of argument would never hold up in a court of law. The job of the judicial system is to find physical evidence and make judgments based on that evidence. However, apart from that system, this trial takes place daily.

Perhaps we have had a medical emergency that has left our resources depleted and our rent is due in three days. Court is in session! As jurors always on duty, we have to choose whose argument we will believe and in whom we have faith. Satan, the prosecutor says, "Look at the evidence! There isn't enough money to pay the bill now and there won't be for two more weeks! There is no one who can loan that much money and if they could, would they? No! This poor landlord needs his money now; can't you see the only verdict is guilty and the only remedy — **eviction**!" Satan constantly presents us with false evidence and draws false conclusions for us. He wants us to live *by* sight and *in* fear.

Fortunately, God speaks for the defense, "The situation is not what is seems. Don't judge based on what you see or what you think you know about it, but on what you have come to know about Me. I will not suffer thy foot to be moved: he that keepeth thee will not slumber. (Psalm 121:3)." God wants us to trust Him, ignore what we see and make our decisions based on FAITH; to "live by faith, not by sight" (2 Corinthians 5:7).

The miracles in this section are testaments to the wonders of active faith. Faith is more than belief in God's power and authority over everything in Heaven and on Earth. It is trusting, surrendering to, and obeying God *based* on that belief. When we do these three, we receive victory!

To accept this truth, we need a relationship with God —

the Father, Son and Holy Spirit. Without the relationship there can be no trust, without trust there can be no surrender, without surrender there can be no obedience, and without obedience there is no victory.

We need to be able to trust Him; sometimes for long periods of time after our request is made. Some miracles of faith have instant results, like the healing of the woman with the issue of blood (Luke 8:43-48) and the restoration of sight to blind Bartimaeus (Mark 10:46-52). At other times, God has called people to persevere in faith, as with the two blind men who follow Jesus, calling to him (Matthew 9:27-30) or the Canaanite woman who asks Him to heal her daughter (Matthew 15: 21-28). In these cases, those in need sought the Lord in persistent faith before their miracle occurred.

Often while we are waiting in faith, doubt comes. One form of doubt is what I call the *"If* Syndrome." Once I was considering all the "ifs" in a situation when the Holy Spirit spoke to me: *"If* backwards is *Fi. Fi* means faithful (in Latin). When you turn your 'if's into *faithfulness*, God will work it out!"

Active faith will move mountains and calm storms in our lives; sometimes in an instant, at other times we must wait. "And without faith it is impossible to please God, because anyone who comes to him must believe that he exists and that he rewards those who earnestly seek him" (Hebrews 11:6).

In each of the following stories, God called people to act in faith, or wait in faith, for a miracle. They trusted in God and brought back a verdict of 'not guilty' in their trial. As your next court date nears, what will be your verdict?

"If you abide in me, and my words abide in you, you can ask what you will and it shall be done unto you."

- John 15:7

Angela Imani - Joseph Montrel

Now in the natural, miracles make us smile. They make us glow with astonishment. They cause us to cry tears of joy, and relief, and to sing praises and thanksgiving to God for what He has done. At least that's the way it's been with any miracles I have ever experienced, read about, or heard. The God I serve walked my husband and me through the strangest phenomena in 1994 — the miracle of life in the birth of our daughter Imani. I cannot describe the joy of expectation in the months prior to her untimely birth. Oh yes, we had to seek God's help in calling down the fears and worries associated with the whole process. Little did I realize, however, that as a result of her extremely early and complicated arrival due to toxemia, I would ultimately have to accept a miracle brought about by her death.

Before she left us, after ten days of a courageous fight, her tiny body, which her nurse could embrace in the palm of her hand, signaled the miraculous power of God and how He orchestrates His plan for our lives. I remember walking away from the Neonatal Intensive Care unit after the second time I saw her. With my heart heavy, I struggled to praise Him in spite of what I had seen. The idea of a miracle seemed to dim. "God, surely you can't mean for this to happen," I thought. Healthy babies were all around me, and sick ones are here that are sure to recover.

Yes, in the natural, miracles make us smile. Yet all the smiles around me seemed forced. In the days to come, God somehow allowed us to witness and be a part of miracles of "new" life and rebirth in those around us. Sometimes I would say, "Wait a minute, I'm the one that's supposed to be crying here." When someone is hurting and doesn't know Christ as you do, how appropriate it is for you to be able to share an experience that offers them hope. My sister would often ask us how we could deal with this situation. We always explained that it was only through Christ and we tried to show her how He could make her life more positive. She had two healthy children and they too needed to know Christ. How exciting it was for me to find that my sister received Christ a few months after Imani's death. She shared with my mother that she had gained a new perspective on her life due to the strength we were able to show during that time.

My mother said to me one day that whatever it cost for Imani's birth and care while on this earth my sister's salvation was worth every penny. Oh I've spent a good amount of time aching inside, and awaking in the middle of the night with tears streaming down my cheeks. I thank God for a husband who loves the Lord, because in the midst of our storm, we could call on Jesus together and know that He would hear us. God's plan may not have been my plan, but I thank Him for His patience with me, as He slowly revealed, piece by piece and day by day by day by day, that He knew what was best. We may not ever fully understand Him, for who knows the mind of God, and what a task it is to learn to trust when things don't make sense.

At my six-week check up, my doctor told me that he believed that if I tried to conceive again, the chances of losing the next child because of toxemia were about 99%. I got a second opinion and was told that the chances would be closer to 25 - 50% that I would become ill again.

So in the natural, miracles make us smile. The miracle of Imani made us trust. It made us hope. It urged us to seize the opportunity to witness the "miracle working" God we served, even when our hearts were heavy. When our hearts were sad (we called it having an "Imani day"), whether bouncing back was quick or time consuming, the Lord was faithful to remind us that He understood and that He loved us. One morning in Sunday School, a brother in Christ shared the scripture: "For we have not an high priest which cannot be touched with the feeling of our infirmities..." (Hebrews 4:15). He will probably never know how much that scripture has pierced my very being and reaffirmed my knowledge of God's love for his saints.

I also thank God for a dear brother and sister in Christ who shared with us a book, which talked about the experience of a woman and her husband who loved the Lord, and desired children. This couple had attempted to have children and conceived four times; each time there was a miscarriage. The wife was diagnosed with an incontinent uterus but believed that it was in God's will for her to have a child. She and her husband came into agreement and were led to research scriptures about conception, and stories about women in the Bible who were told they could not conceive who eventually did. They researched the scriptures and stories of faith in that area. They stood on His word for their miracles of life and as a result they had four healthy children.

I found that I could not only ask for the safe delivery of a healthy baby, but I could ask for the most specific, minute details regarding this child and rest assured that nothing would be too hard for my God. So I did it! I asked for everything from no morning sickness or swollen ankles, to my child having a calm and loving spirit. My husband and I are loving witnesses that God is able to do even above what we hope for.

It's true that in the natural, miracles make us smile. I am smiling. On March 11, 1996, God presented us with another miracle of life. His name is Joseph Montrel. Joseph, meaning, "God shall increase"; Montrel, meaning, "that which cannot be come against." I thank God for the miracles of His word and an uncomplicated delivery of a slightly premature, but very healthy and lively child.

Now they say miracles make us smile - and hope, and believe, and trust and cry... And in death, His miraculous nature can still astound us. Death in Christ means abundant life, and life ever after. No pain can possibly be worse than death for one who is separated from God. "Lord just let me rest in your loving arms and be assured that you know, and will do, what is best for me; and that you will never leave or forsake me." Now THAT makes me smile.

> "And the prayer offered in faith will make the sick person well; the Lord will raise him up."
>
> - James 5:15

An Issue of Blood

During a recent stay in the hospital for a brief illness, I experienced a miracle. I had been at home sick for almost two weeks with severe symptoms after being misdiagnosed by two doctors on two separate occasions. When I continued to get sicker, I went to see a third doctor who realized that my illness was severe enough to admit me to the hospital. While at home, and even while in the hospital, I passed a lot of blood, which caused my blood level to become critically low. The doctor ordered a blood transfusion to rebuild my system and told me the downsides of receiving donated blood: as much as they screen for AIDS and Hepatitis, you may not see any signs until 5 or 10 years later.

I became somewhat troubled, because of what the doctor had told me and because of the risks involved when you receive blood from a donor other than yourself.

When the nurse entered my room to prepare me for the transfusion, I asked her if she would give me a little time to talk all of this over with God. She understood and told me that she would come back in a little while. The phone rang, and it was my pastor. I relayed my concerns to him and he told me he was on his way. Sister Mabry, a registered nurse and member of our church, also called during this time, and she comforted me with some reassuring words, both medically and spiritually. I had to drink during the night to clean out my system and told Sister Mabry. She said the church had lifted me up in prayer that God was ultimately in control. She also told me it was possible that what they had given me may have caused my blood to drop lower. By this time, my husband had come, and I told him that the doctor was adamant that I receive blood. Then my pastor and his wife entered my room.

"We need to pray," he said.

Everyone held hands and formed a circle around me and my pastor went down on bended knee to pray to God about the blood issue. After our prayer time, Pastor patted my leg and told me that everything would be okay. At that moment, I knew no matter what, even if I did receive the blood, everything *would* be okay.

While we were talking, the nurse came back into the room to draw another sample of blood.

"Mrs. Saunders, your doctor said we cannot put this off any longer."

About thirty minutes later, the same nurse came running into my room.

"Your blood has gone up! Blessed be the Lord, you do not need that blood now!"

As weak as I was, I started rejoicing in my hospital bed, praising my Lord for what he had done. Hallelujah!

> "We wait in hope for the LORD;
> he is our help and our shield."
>
> - Psalm 33:20

The Job

My wife and I had just been married, and she was already placed in a counseling position with the school system in southwest Virginia. I had stayed in Charlottesville, and taught in Buckingham County for a year after we were married, because I didn't feel like the Lord had led me to go there yet. A year before I moved, we had decided to fill out an application with the school district there, just to be considered. In the following year, we reactivated the application and I asked the Lord if he would allow me to go and be with my wife.

All systems were 'go' except for a job. So, I decided, "Okay, I'm going, and I'll interview."

There were two high schools in the city, Pickett and Central. We had passed by Central High School on several occasions when I had come to visit. My wife would always say the same thing.

"That's the 'private' public school, and you probably won't ever get a teaching job there because there are not enough African-American students there to warrant hiring another black teacher. So you'll probably work at Pickett if you work at a high school, OR you'll work in an elementary school in art." In my heart I didn't want that.

"I'll take whatever I need to take in order to be here."

Well, it just so happened that when I came to interview for a job there was an opening; and the opening was at the very high school that she said there would probably not be a job for ME.

So, I went and I interviewed. I thought I did a very good interview. The principal liked me. We talked about a lot of things; I came with a list of questions, and we had a nice session. When I left, he told the secretary to make sure she jotted down my name and got my telephone number and he said would be calling me, probably the next day.

"It looks very favorable!" he said.

I thought "Great!" Principals usually don't say it looks 'favorable' to you because they don't want to give you a clue one way or the other. So, I got back in the car and went back to Charlottesville, thinking "I'll wait for the call tomorrow." The next morning I got a call from the city school system.

"Mr. Nicholson, we regret to inform you that the job that you applied for at Central High School has been filled by someone within the system. And so we don't have that position open anymore." I was very sad, so I stopped and prayed.

"Lord, you know I want to be with my wife, why? Why?"

And in my spirit His voice kept saying, "Go. Just go. Start packing up your things and go."

All I could think was I truly didn't want to go, I also was going through this manhood thing. 'I need to be able to provide for my wife. She's already making good money and I'm going to go there....' And He said, "Go."

"Okay," I sighed.

So after I prayed I got up and I said out loud, "If I have to work at McDonald's, I'm going to be with my wife!" And then I thought to myself, "Ugh... I really don't want to go with no job." Then I said out loud again, "If I have to work at McDonald's, I'll go. I'll go."

About an hour later, I got another phone call.

"Mr. Nicholson, even though we do not have the job open at Central, the teacher who filled that position left an opening at Pickett High School. However, it is two elementary schools part time and one high school part time." Again I was thinking 'I don't want to do elementary.' I didn't want to teach elementary school, so I prayed again.

"Lord... elementary..."

And then the Lord came to me and just spoke again, "Go." And in my spirit I said, "Well you know Lord, this woman who applied for the job at Central may have been a Christian, and she may be more capable of teaching high school than I am. Or it may be hard for her to teach elementary school, and I CAN. So, if you know both of us, you know which one of us is more equipped for which job. So I'll trust you. I'll go interview for this job; I'll be with my wife. I won't be working at McDonald's. Praise YOU God!"

I left that next morning and told my wife I was coming. She was very happy. I got there, drove to Pickett High School and walked in the principal's office.

"Have you heard?!" he said.

"Yeah, I'm supposed to interview for this job."

"Yes you are. BUT...did you know that the woman who took the job at Central resigned?"

"What do you mean she resigned?!"

"She decided to take a job in Blacksburg with her husband.

So now the position is open at Central. But the principal over there seems to be so excited about you, that I want to interview you for Pickett."

I interviewed for the job and when I got ready to leave, he said, "I want you at Pickett. I think you would do a great job here. We need more black male role models, please take the position."

"Well, I need to pray about this," I said and he agreed to wait. I went to the school board office.

When I got there, they told me that the principal at CENTRAL had decided that he was going to get me! He had interviewed me first, and the contract was already written and signed. But the amazing thing is that not only did I have A job, I had an opportunity to CHOOSE which job I wanted!

The principal at Pickett had even told me "Go look at the schedule and decide which courses you want to teach!"

So God is good! And he does work miracles! The odds and chances of all that stuff happening... and in the course of two days! But I was willing to yield my spirit to him. I finally said, "Lord, I'm going, you told me to go."

"Faith is the substance of things hoped for, the evidence of things not seen" (Hebrews 11:1). I couldn't see any kind of way, but I went ... and there it was. A miracle.

> *"And it is I who have created the destroyer to work havoc; no weapon forged against you will prevail, and you will refute every tongue that accuses you."*
>
> - Isaiah 54: 16-17

To Crack and Back

I had a miracle happen to me in 1987. It was what got me clean. I was a hustler. I started out with little stuff when I was about 12 and then just kept going. At 22, I had money, houses, cars, even a plane. Then I started to use the stuff I was slinging and I became an addict. I was 28 when it fell apart. My miracle happened when I was frantic, on a three day drug binge smoking Cocaine. I was in turmoil. My father had died a few months back; everything was coming down. It was the worst experience I had ever had.

I was at my mom's house and I was broken up because I was going through all this stuff. I was crying and praying and doing everything that I knew to do spiritually. I was praying to God and asking my mom what to do. I was just crying out for help. I was talking to her and she said "God is right here in this house, right now." She was trying to show me the way.

I was in my dad's room and sure enough God was there. He wasn't picturesque like a man or anything, but there was a Light, a spiritual person, in the corner. And between the Light and me was the Devil. And he was jumping all around, crazily like a monkey. He was trying to stay between me and that Light; trying to block out that Light. But the Light was just shining through him. I was so confused and going through so much, and I just asked God to help me. I could see Him standing there with His arms folded on His chest.

"Look at that Fool."

He was talking about the Devil, who was still running around and jumping all over. "Now, you see this fool?" I just sat there, broken down. "You know how powerful I am, right? I could knock him out of your life right now with just a brush of my hand."

I was crying like a baby. "Well do it! Why don't you do it!? Knock him out!"

"Look, let me tell you something," He was saying. "I could do that." He was trying to explain it to me. "But, I won't do that. Because if I do that, you would be too fanatical." Can you imagine God saying someone could be too fanatical? He was explaining to me that I was already aggressive and on the edge. And he was showing me that if He knocked that Devil down and showed me how strong He was, I would be the kind of person who went off the deep end religiously. I would be addicted again. It was plain. I couldn't believe it, but I had total understanding. He went on.

"I am just leaving you a message right now to let you know that the Devil doesn't have any power over you." He just told me that, straight up.

"He don't have no *power* over me?" I was just tripping.

"He's got no power over you. I can take Him out anytime I want. All I want to see you do is make an effort toward wanting to change your life in this Light that I've got here." Then both of them were gone.

Miracles to Confirm Faith

I could hear my mom talking to me, asking me to get in the bathtub. I did and started to calm down. I still couldn't believe what had happened.

Believe it or not, I got high some more after that time! But it was never the same. That experience led me to sobriety. I never went through that frantic turmoil again. Eventually, I got myself together. It wasn't an event; it was a process. A slow process. I was working at recovery; I got more strength and God just built me up.

I look at myself now. I've been sober since June 1988. I've got my life in order, I've got a wife and a new baby boy. I have had success in business. It's just all different.

I don't tell many people that story because they think I'm crazy. But I believe in God, I know I can just get on my knees and talk to Him. I just know my own relationship with God, because He changed my life *personally*.

Section III:
Miracles to Demonstrate Jesus as Lord and Saviour

55 Miracles to Demonstrate Jesus as Lord and Saviour

"Come, follow me," Jesus said, "and I will make you fishers of men." At once they left their nets and followed him.

- Matthew 4:19-20

The prophets of the Old Testament predicted to Israel that one day a King was to come who would establish himself as their Lord and deliverer. The expectation was that this King would be an earthly lord, who would rule by might and exclusion, not by mercy and acceptance. Jesus reversed the definition of greatness by becoming lowly and showing the intense power of humility, service, and obedience to God. Through these means, he became Lord to all those who would accept him as Saviour, one who would rescue us from lives aimed toward destruction. In his Lordship over both Jews and Gentiles, Jesus showed impartiality and paved the way for unity among all those who believe on his name.

Jesus is Lord, but does not lord it over us as the Biblical Gentile lords did (Matthew 20:25). Rather, he peruses a personal relationship with each of us through which he leads us to everlasting life. The stories you are about to read show how a personal relationship with Jesus as Lord and Saviour has made a difference in the lives of the narrators. We are not alone. As Lord, he has all authority over us; as Saviour, he protects our souls. His dual roles give him dominion to correct and instruct as well as to deliver and preserve.

In comparison to the sacrifice He made, Jesus asks little of us in return for his love and protection. He asks that we follow his example - that we love the Lord our God with all our hearts, and with all our soul, and with all our mind, and that we love our neighbors as ourselves (Matthew 23:37-39). He demands this because when we love God with our hearts, the center of our being, our motives are pure and we seek to do His will (Matthew 5:8). We "hear (his) words and put them into practice" (Luke 6:46-48). Did not the Lord say, "If you love me, you will obey what I command" (John 14:15)? What does He command?

"My command is this: Love each other as I have loved you" (John 15:12). Jesus showed his love by giving up his position to be mocked and scourged (Matthew 27:29-30) that we might receive Life through him. He who is greatest of all, became least of all (Philippians 2:5-7), out of love. In like fashion, we are charged to consider ourselves servants, both to the Lord and to each other (Matthew 20:26-28). We are to let the light of Jesus shine through us into the lives of those around us, encouraging them to seek out the source of our love.

Are we willing to give up our position to rescue another, out of love? "Greater love has no one than this, that he lay down his life for his friends" (John 15:13). Are we willing to relinquish unholy living, to be an example to our friends, out of love?

Love one another. This one command seems simple on the surface, yet it is the full scope of the message that we must heed. The succession of instruction from the Gospel of Luke 6: 27-45 reveals the depth of this message. In verses 27 -36, Christ commands not only that we love those who we approve, but also that we love our enemies. We are instructed to "do good to those who hate (us) and bless those who curse (us)." In verses 37-42, we are warned not to judge, but to forgive and to carefully scrutinize our own lives. The love we are to offer is to be shared with *all* people in a spirit of service to the risen Christ and unconditional forgiveness for those who wrong us. Finally, in verses 43-35, Jesus tells the parable of the tree and its fruit, to remind us that the most powerful tool of our faith is our walk - that which people see in our actions and hear in our words.

As servants of Christ, we must ask ourselves what type of fruit we bear. Is it embittered with envy, jealousy, gossip, and judgment? Or is it sweetened with love, joy, peace, patience, kindness, goodness, faithfulness, gentleness and self-control (1 Corinthians 13:4-5, Galatians 5:22-23)? No, we cannot succeed alone. We need a vine in which to abide (John 15:4), a personal Lord and Saviour to live in us, speak for us, hear us and redeem us. We have this, and infinitely more in Jesus Christ, when we choose to answer his call - "Follow me."

> "*Humble yourselves, therefore, under God's mighty hand, that he may lift you up in due time. Cast all your anxiety on him because he cares for you.*"
>
> - 1 Peter 5:6-7

In God's Hands

I became sick in 1991 and when the doctors said I had to have surgery, I just fell apart. I was nervous and it was just chaos. I went through that surgery without faith. I knew God but I just didn't have that much faith; you know it takes faith to build faith. After the surgery I hemorrhaged. I lost so much blood, the doctors thought they would have to give me a transfusion. I was so sick, I was off work five months. I was so stressed out. My husband wasn't saved and didn't want the church family around. At that time, I depended on people, not God. I had not turned my situation over to God and it was just bad.

In 1995, I went to the doctor for a check up. He felt my stomach and looked at me.

"Janie, what's wrong with you?"

"Nothing. I just gained a few pounds."

"Your stomach is hard as a brick! You look six months pregnant. Are you pregnant?" He was worried.

"No, I'm not pregnant. I just gained weight."

"No, there's something there."

A year before the doctors had told me there was 'something there' but when they did tests, they couldn't find anything. They did more tests and this time they found a tumor. I went back so they could see if it had grown. On Friday, December 9th, the doctor called again.

"Janie, you have to have surgery."

"Okay."

"You have to have it Tuesday."

I said, "You can wait until after Christmas can't you?"

"You'll be dead if you wait until after Christmas, you've got to have it now."

When I got off the phone, I thought, go pick up the phone and call someone. "No," I said, so I went into the living room and I talked to God.

"God, you know my situation," I said. " You know. You know what I need to have done. I'm putting this in your hands." You see, my mother had the same thing years ago. Her tumor grew so fast, that it poisoned her before they could do anything. It killed her. She was only 49. And I was 40 then. I said, " I'm not going to dwell on that. God, I'm putting this in your hands." And I didn't talk about it anymore.

You know people say they put things in God's hands, but they really don't! You put it in His hands and then you try to deal with it yourself! I had learned since 1991 how to leave it in His hands.

That Tuesday, I went to the hospital. I got there and I prayed about the surgery again. I was just so happy. I started thinking that maybe somebody would see my light shine through this. Maybe this surgery would bring someone to God.

"God," I said. "When I go in today, let me be a witness. Use me. Everything I do I want you to be in the midst of it." And He was, from the time I left my house until the time I got home.

My husband, brother and daughter were at the hospital with me and I was reading Psalm 21, when they told me it was time to go. "I will lift mine eye unto the hills, from whence cometh my help. My help cometh from the Lord, which made heaven and earth."

They were going to take me for surgery prep early, so my pastor had not gotten there yet. My family was worried about it. I was fine.

You know, you don't have to have the pastor there to pray for you when you're a Christian. You can pray for yourself. God hears *your* prayers.

I had a peace within me that I had never had. When they came in to prep me the lady asked me if someone had given me a pep pill.

"I've got Jesus!"

"But you're so happy!" she said.

"I'VE got JESUS!"

And I was thinking, doesn't anybody know that there is a God?

I was ready to go to surgery, when someone said, "You can't go down yet, your pastor is here." So they rolled me back to the room and he came in.

That lifted my spirits even more, but if he hadn't gotten there I was all right, because I had God. God was in the midst of everything!

After surgery, the doctor came in and said, "Janie, you're doing fine, there was no cancer."

"Thank God," I said. But if there *had* been cancer, I STILL had God.

The next day the doctor said, "Janie, I could tell that everybody was praying for you. Prayers were sent up. I could feel it in my hands. I have done surgery on you before; this time you were so relaxed."

Friday, when I was going to leave the hospital, a man from work, who had dealt with some nervous problems the year before, called.

He said, "Janie, are you okay?" I told him I was doing fine.

"I want to tell you this," he said. "You know you kept me going last year. You sent me cards and prayed and I didn't know there was a God until then. You talk about God so much. You always pray for us at work. And I see God in you." He started crying. "Janie, you don't know how much I prayed for you. You know I don't pray. I've never prayed for anyone like I prayed for you."

"You know what?" I said, "My surgery was worth having, because you've seen God."

That's when I knew it happened for a reason. It happened to show what can happen when you put God in control. It made my faith so much stronger. And I changed. This time I listened to the doctor and I didn't do anything I wasn't supposed to. I just rested and I was out of the house in three weeks. This time I healed better and faster. I didn't get sick, because I put it in His hands. Sometimes you have to go through valleys to appreciate the mountains. But all you have to do is put it in God's hands.

> "On the third day he will rise again."
>
> -Luke 18:33

Miracles of Three

Three months after I was born, I developed asthma. I was in the hospital at least every week or so. Mom said the doctors told her this was a chronic illness; this was something her child would have to live with. So every week, my mom took me to the doctors and I got shots.

Back then they didn't a lot of drugs to give children for asthma, so I was a sickly child. I remember my mother just sitting up and rocking me sometimes. When I turned *three*, I got very sick. I had some type of virus and my lungs were weakening. The doctors came to my mom and dad and told them that I would not live through the night. My dad would just not accept this.

When I was born, Dad told my mother "This child is going to be special." I was the *ninth* child in our family, and the only child that my father had wanted to name, and he took a long time to name me.

My Mom said my Dad disappeared that night after the doctors left and was gone all night long. That next morning they were giving me oxygen and I was holding on. Night came again and my dad was still gone. When the third night came, I was still holding on. On the *third* day, my dad came back, walked into the room and told my mother that I was going to live.

After that, I started getting better and better until I was fully recovered. I was able to stop taking medication when I was twelve. I know it is a miracle that I lived, but I don't know what happened or what he did those three days. But it makes me feel good when I think about it. It makes me feel special that he didn't give up on me.

And because of whatever he did in that three days in the third year of my life, I went on to become a state sprinter. Ironically, I won states for *three years* in a row.

> For God, who said, "Let light shine out of darkness,"
> made his light shine in our hearts to give us the light of the
> knowledge of the glory of God in the face of Christ.
>
> - 2 Corinthians 4:6

The Monkey

In 1988, I was in the terminal stages of my drug addiction and the circumstances of my life were forcing me to make a decision to cross the line and be a total reprobate or to take an opportunity to hear what God was saying in my life. At the end of 1988, I was so miserable and so empty and suffering from so much guilt about the terrible things I had done, that I began to go to the Veterans Hospital for help. The first time I went, my six foot plus frame was at 167 pounds. I was totally dehydrated and near death. They nursed me back to health and I picked up some weight. But once I got out I went straight to the drugstore, or the pusher, and continued using drugs.

I began to get sick of that life and tried to stop it by isolating myself in my home and not going out at all. After about a week, I was so psychotic I was seeing things, hearing things, and thinking someone was in the house. I would get up in the middle of the night and search through the closets, but nobody was really there. Finally, I would go out and start using again. I was in a cycle.

I went to the Veterans Hospital for a second time. The people in the emergency room brought a psychiatrist in to see if I was suicidal. At first I thought that an absurd question, but then I realized I had been committing suicide all along. I was just on a payment plan - a little at a time.

In February of 1989, when I was released from the hospital, I sought a reference from them for a treatment program. The one they suggested was the best in the state, but the program began in April.

"I'll be dead by then," I confessed.

They sent me to another facility where I could begin immediately. I remember thinking "What should I take with me?" and I thought of the Bible my aunt had given me. As a child, I was taught Christianity by my parents. Now the idea of God was attractive to me again. I knew with drugs I had been under the influence of a higher power, that I had given control of my life to something that was very evil and that stripped me of any self-worth at all.

During the course of my treatment I expressed my addiction experiences through drawings. The addiction was usually a monkey. A small monkey holding needles. A monkey trapped in a cage. Me walking down a winding road, thinking of needles, passing under a cloud raining needles, with monkeys at each end of the road. Finally, the monkey grew to the size of King Kong, overwhelming, like the addiction.

On Easter, while in treatment, I had a revelation. Each year a local seminary would send ministers in training to conduct Easter Sunday service at the center. This particular year, the signals got crossed and no one thought there would be a service, so all the patients had been released to other activities. Twelve pastors and the Chaplain showed up. Out of 75 patients, I was the only one there.

During the long discussion with them, I Realized that people make mistakes, that everyone had a particular sin. No one should look down me because I was a drug addict, because they also had sins. After the meeting one of the visitors approached me.

"Would you come speak to my church in the next few weeks?" he asked. Then another came. And another. My answer was very honest.

"I need to see if I am going to live or die. I don't know what's going to happen when I leave here." There was that much uncertainty in my life.

They were surprised to discover that I was a patient. They had thought I was an assistant to the chaplain!

Then came the revelation. No matter where I was at that time, if I gave myself to God, there was no telling where I would end up! The answer was to "Let go and let God." Once I did that, I got a glimpse of what had been hidden all along. The evil, the sin, the drug addiction in my life had become such a fixture that I could not see anything beyond it. There was King Kong, his giant back facing me and blocking out the future. I could not imagine life without it, or him. Now I realized the truth: that I was an unwilling participant in this thing. I had willingly given myself to it, but I wanted to get out. I didn't know how, nor could I do it on my own. Then I had a vision of something I could not describe nor fully comprehend.

I knew it was infinitely good, it was loving and kind. I knew I had to be patient for more to be revealed. But the vision remained.

I drew the picture of Kong again, only this time I could see something beyond him. I drew a light that was far away and yet even at that distance, it was larger than the monstrous addiction. More and more I thought about God being what I needed to redeem myself. Because of my upbringing I always connected God with the Bible, so I tried to just pick it up and read, even though I did not understand it.

In the mornings I would just say "God, help me get through this day." At night I would thank Him. These were probably the most powerful prayers I have prayed to date and he kept His word. He got me through it. In July of 1989 I accepted Christ as my personal Saviour.

When I left the treatment center, I was searching for guidance and support to help me continue toward that light. I tried a few groups, but I didn't get what I needed. In December of 1989, a friend told me about a church and its pastor; so, I visited. Nothing stuck out or impressed me the first time I went, but since my friend often went, I decided to visit again with him.

The next time, Sunday school had been canceled and there were some people still there, so they held class. I was impressed that a group of people could conduct things without the pastor being present. I continued to attend and in February of 1990 I met my wife there. We fast became engaged and were married in September.

My life at there has been one blessed with tremendous growth. When my wife and I married, I was unemployed, going to school. By God's grace, we made it through. In 1993, I started to teach in a local school district and I am seeing opportunities open up there too. Today I am involved in a master's program and my life has just exploded. To God be the Glory.

> *"Lord," they answered, "we want our sight."*
> *Jesus had compassion on them and touched their eyes.*
> *Immediately they received their sight and followed him."*
>
> *- Matthew 21:33-34*

...But Now I See

This miracle is only one of many in my life. First, let me tell you I am diabetic and have been through a lot because of my condition. A few years ago, my vision became blurred and that scared me a lot. Since I have diabetes, I was supposed to be getting my eyes checked regularly all along, but I wasn't. When I finally went to the doctor there were some problems and the resident told me I should go to a specialist. He suggested a doctor at a local Clinic where the doctors specialize in eyes, ears, nose and throat. She took x-rays of my eyes. We looked at the x-rays and I saw that some of the tissue had disappeared from my eyes. The doctor didn't have much hope for my sight to return.

I prayed and cried, at home, at church, at work and at the hospital, that Dr. Jesus would hear me. I asked my church family for prayer too. My doctor at the clinic said I could get reading glasses and also suggested laser surgery, but she didn't know if that would help. Well, I believe that doctor was an instrument of God; she knew what to do, and she was very compassionate. She really cared that I was scared. Just knowing that I could have my eyes operated on without being cut was miraculous. People a long time ago weren't that fortunate. I had the laser surgery done on my eyes to help me see better and I started wearing reading glasses.

Well, a couple of months later she took more x-rays of my eyes. I looked at them and saw that God had fixed the tissue! Now I still wear glasses but my vision has returned! Even with my diabetes, I haven't had any more problems with my vision and I will continue to trust Jesus for my eyesight. I am thankful for Jesus, my families at home and at church and I thank God I still have *and will continue to have* my sight in Jesus' name! Praise God!!

Section IV:

Miracles To Advance the Gospel

73 Miracles to Advance the Gospel

> *"Calling the Twelve to him, he sent them out two by two and gave them authority over evil spirits."*
>
> — Mark 6:7

"In the beginning was the Word, and the Word was with God, and the Word was God" (John 1:1). Throughout history, God has found ways to share the good news of His word, His salvation, and His truth. One way has been through the Bible; another, through 'ordinary' people like you and me, sent out to carry His message. But how ordinary are we, *really*?

"... God created man *in his own image, in the image of God* he created him; male and female he created them" (Genesis 1:27). Adam, Eve and all people since, were created in God's image. Certainly nothing about our Maker nor our purpose is ordinary! We are extraordinary creatures, made in the likeness of an extraordinary Spirit. Our purpose: to make known His presence on earth.

During the creation, God passed on his blessed nature to his children. However, He did not gift all aspects of His nature to either being, but instead divided his attributes among the two: a son, Adam and a daughter, Eve.

As you will read, many of God's sons and daughters proclaim the 'good news' as individuals; and yet, that is only part of the plan He intended. Because his image was divided between man and woman at the Creation, that image is not whole unless *we* are one. So, God created marriage, that we again "become one flesh" (Genesis 2:24, Mark 10:6-9) and fully reflect His image. This perfect union of man and woman, conceived in the Garden of Eden, is a powerful ingredient in advancing the Gospel.

Christ sent disciples to all parts of the earth in *pairs* to spread the gospel (Mark 6:7, Luke 10:1). In like manner, God pairs us, with our spiritual gifts in mind, to do the same. When we are baptized in the Holy Spirit we receive our spiritual gifts (1 Corinthians 12:4-11). God desires spiritual partnerships for us wherein one spouse's gifts compliment the gifts of the other.

It is through this oneness that God gives us the power to perpetuate life, both in flesh and in spirit. When we become one *in flesh*, we are empowered to procreate, to produce children in flesh. Similarly, when we as a couple are one *in spirit*, we are empowered to bring forth new Life in others, through spiritual rebirth.

I know a couple in which the husband is very sociable and outgoing. He invites people to his church and his home and is a consummate host. He opens the doors to interaction. His wife is a teacher and exhorter. She directs and encourages those around her in their faith walk. She lights the path for spiritual rebirth and growth. Separately, the operation of their gifts is incomplete; in combination, their ministry of salvation is whole.

God's perfect plan is that couples be one, and one in nature with Him. We are a team. Ideally, a man and woman are 'fitly joined' together in their gifts and go into the world to mirror God's image; just as the disciples went out two by two to represent Jesus, and as the church, with its combined gifts, goes into the world to personify the "body of Christ" (Ephesians 4:16).

The union God desires for us is that of three: male, female, and God. Marriage, then, can be illustrated through the triangle. Think of God as the apex, or uppermost point, and man and woman as the two points on the base. The lines are the relationships that bind them to each other. Among triangles, the most stable is the equilateral, where the two sides connecting each point to the apex are equal in length. Equal sides are symbolic of our relationships with God being the same or similar. The closer you as points move toward God, the closer you will also get to each other!

Some may then ask, 'What about unsaved partners, or single people?' In both cases the believer is to rely on God as divine spouse. When one partner is unsaved, half of the gifts and one side of the triangle are missing. There is no stability and there is no wholeness in God. That is why God does not approve of marriages between believers and non-believers (2 Corinthians 6:14).

Single believers too have a sanctified marriage with God. When they depend on their divine spouse, they can have a strong ministry based on that union with God. Jesus and Paul, as single men, are examples of the power that can exist in a marriage of the two.

Whichever situation you are in, your ministry is important and unique. God desires us as his children and his partners to make the most of the gifts and the time he has given us to reflect His image, spread His Word, and create New Life.

"Therefore go and make disciples of all nations, baptizing them in the name of the Father and of the Son and of the Holy Spirit, and teaching them to obey everything I have commanded you. And surely I am with you always, to the very end of the age" (Matthew 28:19-20).

Have you sought God's will for you in ministry?

> "Then said Jesus unto him, Except ye see signs and wonders, ye will not believe."
>
> - John 4:48

Signs and Wonders

We were traveling from Indiana to Detroit on a beautiful sunny day. My husband, Roy, was driving and I was sitting in the front passenger seat silently praying and asking God what He had for me to do: what my mission was. He showed me a vision of myself speaking before many people. After the vision, I saw with my natural eyes a service station ahead.

"When we get to the service station, it's going to rain," I said to Roy. And it did.

About a half mile away, I saw a telephone pole and I said, "When we get there it's going to stop." And it did. This continued five or six times and finally Roy asked me to stop telling him about it. I laughed and said, "I don't know why this is happening."

As the months went by, I asked my pastor and several brothers and sisters to explain what it meant, but no one could or did.

A few years passed. I was washing dishes one morning, praying and asking God the same question, "Lord, what do you have for me to do?"

I saw myself once again speaking before many people and I was reminded of the rain. Then the Lord showed me the parallel in what that day meant. When I told Roy it was going to rain, that was like my speaking before people. The rain itself was the 'sign' that my speaking was from God. God was showing me that 'signs and wonders' would follow my ministry. Just like it happened that day, I would speak and a sign would follow, even if we didn't understand why. Out of my mouth would come words that we would not understand but those things would happen. It has taken many years, but I have seen God open many doors and he's already given me speaking engagements. I have seen a few signs and am waiting for more.

I have seen healings of people who had one limb shorter than the other, and whose short limb grew to be equal with the normal limb. I have also experienced the 'word of knowledge,' where God gives you a word that is important at that exact time.

Once I remember receiving a 'word of knowledge' during a Bible study at my house. Right before the study we would always have prayer. I was the one praying on that particular night and I kept hearing the word "feet" while I was praying. I just kept hearing "feet" and I was thinking, "What in the world!?" I kept trying to turn that word off because it made no sense to me. It had nothing to do with the prayer I was praying, or *trying* to pray, but I kept hearing "feet.. feet." After the prayer I didn't know whether I should mention that or not, because it sounded ridiculous to me. Finally, I said to the group, "I keep hearing the word feet!" One of the sisters there said "Feet?!" I've been having foot problems! Pray for my feet!" We prayed for her feet and they were healed!

In the last few months, some other confirmations have occurred. After church one Sunday, I went up to shake the pastor's hand and he said to me "Shirley, you're either going to publicly accept your call or..." I don't remember what he said after that. I think I said to him, "We'll be praying about it." He said, "I've already prayed about it."

About two or three weeks after that, I was in the bathroom getting ready for work and I heard this word in my head: "Nomenclature!" It was very loud. Then I heard it again even louder, "NOMENCLATURE!" And I thought, "What in the world IS that?" I didn't know whether it was a real word or not, but I thought maybe I had heard it before. I wasn't sure, so I thought, well, I'll get the dictionary. I started looking it up as it sounded 'n-a-m-e-n...' and couldn't find it. So I said, "Lord, I don't know what that means. You're gonna have to be more plain than that, because I don't know what it is." And I went to work.

That afternoon I came home, sat down at the kitchen table and began to do some work for school. As I began, I could feel the nudging of the Holy Spirit urging me to pray or to do something spiritual. So I got up and said, "Okay I'm gonna wash some dishes and be praying in the spirit." And I heard it again, "NOMENCLATURE!"

"What in the world is that?" I thought. Just then Roy walked in and I said "Have you ever heard of a word called nomenclature?" He looked puzzled and then repeated it, "nomenclature." I asked him to look it up and he found it. One of the definitions was 'a time for naming,' 'name designation.' That 'word' reminded me of what my pastor said about it being time for me to publicly accept my call. Before that, I hadn't wanted to put a name to it.

Another two weeks passed and I was back in my little office at the house. Once again I was doing some schoolwork, and again I heard the urgings of the Holy Spirit, so I got up and just start praising the Lord. I was praying and thanking Him but I couldn't get a release. The more I prayed and praised Him, the more I felt the same. It was like I wasn't hearing what God wanted me to hear.

Finally I said "Lord, I don't know what you want." So I gave up and sat back down. "I'm going back to work, I don't know what you're saying." As I was working, I was writing a word, a simple word: 'posses'. Now, I know how to spell 'possesses', but at that moment I was thinking, how many 'S's are in possesses? I was working on a legal document so I thought I better make sure.

I opened the dictionary and the first word that I saw was "pulpit." I was still thinking this was just coincidence, so I wasn't even going to pay any attention to it. As I was about to flip the page to look for 'possesses,' the Holy Spirit said, "Read the definition." I thought I knew what a pulpit was. It's where the preacher stands, or the little podium. But as I read on, one of the definitions I came to was "preaching profession; a preaching position."

I guess a few weeks more went by and I hadn't heard much more from the Lord, so I was questioning. "What are you doing? What are you saying? What do you want?" And the next words I heard from the Lord were, "Be still and know that I am God." And so that's where I am now, resting in Jesus until it is time for my ministry to be fulfilled.

May the God of hope fill you with all joy and peace as you trust in him, so that you may overflow with hope by the power of the Holy Spirit.

Romans 15:13

Calming the Storm

One Christmas, I had something incredible happen to me. It started out not being a very happy holiday, but it ended with God being glorified through a *series* of miracles. Three days before Christmas, I lost a relationship that was very important to me. It ended very abruptly and I was very distraught about it. I started going over and over in my mind what had happened, what had gone wrong, and why, and I was creating a lot of upset about the situation. I called a friend of mine for spiritual help. She tried to give me comfort by telling me to just put it in God's hands and leave it alone because whatever was for the best, would happen and that I needed to trust in that.

About then I made a remark about the wind blowing. It was just howling, like a hurricane. It was the hardest I could remember hearing the wind blow in the middle of the day. She said the wind wasn't blowing where she was, which was strange to me because she just lives about 15 minutes across town.

"Well, it's really blowing over here!" I said.

"You know, you could go outside and stop that wind if you wanted to," she said. I didn't know what to say. "It's true," she said calmly. "Jesus said that we would do everything he did (John

14:12), and he stopped the wind from blowing."

As she was talking, I opened up my Bible to try and find the story about Jesus and the storm. The pages opened to Matthew and the first thing I saw was "The foxes have holes, and the birds of the air have nests; but the Son of man hath nowhere to lay his head" (Matthew 8:20). I started flipping the pages backward.

"Here it is," she said. "Matthew 8:23-27."

It was on the very same page my Bible had opened to. We talked about trust and faith, and I started feeling a lot better. I noticed that the wind had died down, so I told her, thinking it had probably moved to her side of town by now. It hadn't. She asked me what God was doing with the wind. I told her and then she said, "How do you feel?" I felt calmer too. Then I realized that I was living a parable. God was showing me that he can calm any storm, whether it is one raging outside or inside. I felt powerful, secure and comforted. The air was still. I was at peace, and there was peace outside.

The next day I was telling my sister this story and she shared how she had been feeling that God had turned his back on her. I shared some scriptures with her, we talked about how God never leaves or forsakes us, and I prayed openly with her. It was a prayer that was led and spoken by the Holy Spirit. It was a powerful prayer; an appropriate prayer, and it was certainly of God, not me. Afterward, I thought how incredible that was, because I had never been the one anyone turned to in spiritual matters.

The next morning my mother shared with me the stress going on in her life. We shared scripture and prayed. I had never prayed openly for anyone in my family before and within two days it had happened twice. I was excited and just awed that God had decided to use me in those ways.

When I look back, there are so many miracles in all that happened those three days. Not just the wind, but the fact that I was so at peace with my situation. If I had not found peace that day, and had gone home upset, I would have been thinking only about me. I wouldn't have had that testimony to share with my sister and I wouldn't have been sensitive to my mother's need. I just don't think any of that would have happened if I had been concentrating on me: *my* feelings, *my* being hurt and hurting someone else, *my* losing a relationship, 'why this?' and 'why that?' God changed my focus, and because I was able to trust Him, he was able to use me in very powerful ways.

> "Again, I tell you that if two of you on earth agree about anything you ask for, it will be done for you by my Father in heaven."
>
> - Matthew 18:19

Three Sisters

It was time for my family to move to Germany and I didn't want to go. My husband was in the service and I had just found a new fellowship and was growing spiritually.

"I can't go now, Lord!" I didn't *want* to go; I was just so happy and excited about my growth in the Lord. But He said, "I'll be there. I'll be in Germany too."

So off to Germany we went. I couldn't find any Christians; everybody I met asked the same things: "You like to drink? Smoke? Get high? You go to the clubs?"

I couldn't find anybody who wanted to praise the Lord. I remember going to one church in Berlin, and every time I would say 'Amen' or 'Thank you, Lord' everybody would turn around to see who was talking. I knew that wasn't the place that I wanted to be. I asked the Lord to give me *somebody*.

One day I went shopping with a friend and I saw this woman. My friend spoke to her and introduced us. Her name was Laura. We only said hello, but there was something about her that gave me the feeling she was saved. I ran into the same woman at another store that day, not 30 minutes later. I wanted to say something but didn't know what to say. We just passed each other.

"Lord,' I said. "If I see this woman one more time I'm gonna ask her what church she goes to, or if she's saved, or something!" I did see her again and when I finally talked to her, I was so happy because she *was* saved. We began to hug and embrace. Then she asked me, "Is your husband an officer?" I didn't want to answer the question because I had heard that enlisted personnel and the officers were not supposed to mingle.

"Well... does it matter?" I said. "Will it make a difference?"

"No," she said. "But God told me that an officer's wife was coming."

"Well, that's ME!"

So, I began to go to her church. Shortly afterwards, the pastor left and the church disbanded. God told Laura that she, another sister named Cathy, and I, should start having Sunday School for our kids at her house.

We had gone to her big old German house many times before. Up on the third floor, she had a tiny room we called "the upper room." We would go in the upper room and we would pray and praise God and just thank Him. It was there that God told Laura about the Sunday school.

Well, we started the school and soon other women began to bring their children. "Now Lord, we want you to send us some men," we prayed. And we started seeing husbands coming and getting saved. Later, we said, "Lord, we need to move back into the chapel." So Laura got her missionary license and she was able to be our pastor at chapel.

The three sisters, Laura, Cathy and I, got everything started: the choir, the usher board, and the children's church. Everything that a large church would have, we were able to establish. Every detail. And everything just flowed. People were coming and they were getting saved.

Back in the upper room we began to pray again.

"Lord, we want you to send us a pastor."

Sure enough, the Lord sent us a pastor. He was only there for about a month before Laura was transferred. Cathy left the next month. I left the next month. All of us left ahead of schedule; one month after the other.

None of us were supposed to leave at the time we did, but it was as if we had done our work and now it was time to move on.

That's always been a real special memory for me; it shows how God will move with prayer. It doesn't take a lot of people; just two or three gathered in His name, praising him, and lifting him up.

> "My sheep listen to my voice; I know them, and they follow me. I give them eternal life, and they shall never perish; no one can snatch them out of my hand."
>
> *- John 10: 27-28*

Divine Whisperings

While attending a conference, I learned that miracles are not always tremendous feats; sometimes they are merely the whisperings of God captured and acted upon.

I had awakened early and decided to lie in bed and spend some time doing a little reading. I automatically reached for "Celebration of Discipline" by Richard Foster. I started reading and got a few pages along when I came to a sentence that said, "We serve out of whispered promptings, divine urgings."[4] I started to feel again in my spirit that I hadn't really been listening to God lately. I say again because I had prayed the night before that I would be able to hear *Kol Yahweh*, the voice of God.

As I read, I felt encouraged to pray. I started to wonder what to pray about, so I sat up. "Well, I'll just meditate a little sitting here." Then I heard *"Get on your knees and pray."* So I did.

I was trying to pray and not getting anywhere when I remembered that praise opens the door to prayer. I started thanking God for all that had happened at the conference, the people I had met, the beautiful weather, the rest, the fun I was having, and for another conference attendee and friend named Kim. I thanked Him that because of Kim, I was able to focus on actually living in

---

[4] Richard Foster, Celebration of Discipline

the present. Sometimes I would tend get stuck thinking about the future or worrying about the past instead of just living in the moment. Well, the more I praised, the more light shone in my soul. That's the only way I can describe it, other than a smiling something that took hold of my face. I started to sense a presence that was familiar, though it wasn't saying anything.

I wanted to ask some questions about what I should do. I thought about service again, and I asked, "What is my service?" *"Writing"* came back. My first thought was, now am I saying this because that's what I want or is God talking here? So I asked, "Is this just me or are You speaking to me?" The answer returned, *"Yes, it's Me."* I wanted to know more.

"What will I write? When?"

"I will tell you." I still wanted to know when.

A few moments later I heard words come out of my spirit. They were so beautiful! They were speaking of prayer and how a prayer flies on the wings of our breath. And now I could see them, I could see the words flying up to the throne of God and I could see them lighting on His ear like butterflies, softly batting their wings and blowing their requests into the ears of God. As I was seeing and hearing these things, I thought, wait a minute! I need to write this down. I had brought my laptop computer so I rushed over to turn it on.

I continued to listen, and wrote, verbatim, the things I remembered and then others words as I heard them. Out of that came three poems, one of which was very confusing to me. It spoke of Jerusalem, and since I do not have a lot of knowledge of the history of Israel, I didn't understand. But I wrote it down anyway, checking with The Voice for words that seemed out of place and trusting that the ones I did not understand would become clear. They did. What you see below are the whispering and utterances I heard on that morning, in their original forms.

WINGS OF PRAYER [5]
Yes, I will pray unto you
For on the wings of my breath
My words fly up to you
And light on your ear as a butterfly.
My pleasure is your will
And your will, my pleasure
That we shall dwell together for eternity

HEARTSONGS [6]
Cry not unto me Oh, Jerusalem
You call is distant in the night and weeping
Your soul has been stolen by a thousand years of wrongs
Life snuffed as lights from candles
Filling a sanctuary at festival
No tears for me Oh, Jerusalem
Whose fire has burned long past its time
And seeking sorrow will do no harm
I am warm and cool imaginings
Floating to the surface of your minds
As you turn to me for favor
As I turn my head and weep

---

[5] ©1997
[6] ©1997

FLY TO ME [7]
Fly to me with open arms
You are children of my flesh
Warming the Word in ways I cannot
Fly unto me my children
Who are lost and weary and saved
With souls searching for a resting place
And eyes sore from cold winds of life
I am here and with you if you only Reach unto me
Speak to me and love my Word
Give me time and patience and goodness
For all time, not merely today
Fly, fly, FLY!
Take wing and soar among the prophets
Sing new songs of mercy
Delight in me on earth
Show others the way to peace and light
And my love will follow them always.

---

[7] ©1997

Section V:

Miracles to Deliver God's People

Miracles to Deliver God's People

> *"I tell you the truth, anyone who has faith in me will do what I have been doing. He will do even greater things than these, because I am going to the Father."*
>
> -John 14:12

In the preceding four sections of this book you have relived miracles of many kinds and in many voices. The culmination of these sections is in Miracles of Deliverance. I say it is the culmination because the performance and sharing of miracles ideally culminates in the deliverance of an unbeliever from a life without Christ. The miracles that close this book show God's deliverance of His people from death, danger, and defeat. It is also his will that non-believers be delivered.

Just as God has a plan for redeeming the world (Ephesians 1:11-14); he has a plan for the deliverance of the unsaved. This plan can be easily seen in the progression of each topical section of this book. First came **compassion**, then **faith**, then recognition of **Jesus as Lord and Saviour**, then **advancing the gospel**. The final result is **deliverance**.

You are a part of God's plan for the deliverance of others. And in order to carry out the plan you must know how it all fits together: God, in His **compassion**, sent Jesus to earth so that he could live among humanity and that we could experience 'God among us' (Immanuel). Through Jesus we were allowed to "see" God in a way we as humans could understand. God used One seen to lead us to **faith** in One unseen. When Jesus was crucified, he died that we might be freed from condemnation. When he rose, he began his reign as **Lord and Saviour** of the world, that through Christ we could know God's saving nature and his resurrection power. Since that day, he has waited for us to seek Him for our individual salvation; to ask him to be our personal Lord and Saviour. "That if thou shalt confess with thy mouth the Lord Jesus, and shalt believe in thine heart that God hath raised him from the dead, thou shalt be saved" (Romans 10:9). As part of our acceptance of him, we also accept the **responsibility to lead a life that reflects that of Christ and to advance the Gospel as** the apostles did. God ordains each of us as messengers that others, too, may claim **deliverance** through the One who stands to bridge the chasm of sin that separates us from the Father.

You are a miracle waiting to happen, an agent of deliverance with a Guide, a plan, and encouragement to ensure your success. You can show your compassion for a nonbeliever by sharing your faith and introducing him to Jesus, your Lord and Saviour. Your work continues as you advance the Gospel, sharing the Word of God with, and genuinely seeking, the unbeliever's deliverance through prayer and patient persistence.

Miracles performed by Jesus were done expressly to show that God was in Him and He in God, that those who were witnesses would believe. You too have the power to be a conduit for miracles because Christ is in you and you are in Christ. Before he left the disciples, Christ not only explained the significance of miracles performed through Him, but also that we would bring even more glory to God than he, by carrying on the work He began. The only requirement for success is faith in Him (Philippians 4:13). If we ask, He will do the rest.

The redemption plan began with God and continues through each of us. There is a miracle waiting to happen today; and all that's missing is you.

> "He has delivered us from such a deadly peril,
> and he will deliver us. On him we have set our hope
> that he will continue to deliver us,"
>
> - 2 Corinthians 1:10

Station Wagon Revival

It was a Saturday morning the year I was in the tenth grade. My father is a minister and had to preach in Tulsa that day, about thirty minutes away. The church didn't have a van, so when he had to preach somewhere, we had a caravan of cars that would go along. There were at least four cars going that day. Our family had a Chevrolet Impala station wagon at the time and it was filled to capacity. Maybe even one passenger over capacity. There were three people in the front seat, three in the middle seat and four kids in the far back. In those wagons there were two seats in the very back that unfolded to seat four. I was in the Rear of the car with my brothers.

Everyone met at the church and we pulled off toward 75, the highway that goes into Tulsa. There were several people who needed gas, so we pulled over at a gas station off the highway, just at the end of town. When we finished getting our gas, we went down the highway a little and pulled onto the side of the road to wait for the others. We were just talking and doing our thing. Suddenly, my older brother Kevin yelled, "Oh, no!"

The next thing I knew there was this big impact and I heard glass shattering all around me. It all took less than 20 seconds.

When it was over, there was no glass in the back window of the station wagon or on the whole left side. There was broken glass everywhere, and the entire side of the station wagon was crushed.

Kevin, who had been looking out the back window, later told us what he had seen. There was a semi truck, which was headed straight for the back of our station wagon. He didn't have a load on the back, just the cab. The driver apparently had lost control. Kevin said that just before the truck got to the station wagon, he swerved. If he had hit the back of the station wagon there would have been some casualties, at least four, including me.

Nobody was seriously injured. The worst injury anybody had was glass in their face that the doctor had to take out. The glass had broken up into such small pieces, even that wasn't anything serious. It was just wild. And that was the only time, while we were kids, that any of us saw the inside of a hospital. And even then it wasn't a major issue. We often talked about how wild it was that everybody walked away from that accident.

> *"If God is for us, who can be against us?"*
>
> *- Romans 8:31b*

The Investigation

I was working on Good Friday, when the postal inspector called. I thought it a little unusual, but figured it was related to mailings from work. Instead, he was calling about a package he said I had signed for. He asked a lot of questions and then asked me to come talk to him the next Tuesday at 2 o'clock. His tone, made me nervous, so I asked about having a lawyer present.

"Oh, no, this is just an informal thing." he told me. "I will be there and maybe another woman from the office. Nothing to be concerned about, we just have a few questions. But we have to ask you to keep this confidential because we are conducting a very important investigation. You cannot talk to anyone about this." I started to worry.

By Easter Sunday, I was drained from the emotion. Frightening thoughts overran my mind like an untended garden. I thought it best to find someone to go to the meeting with me, and I prayed that God would guide me. I called a friend and he graciously gave me the names of two lawyers. This couldn't be happening to me.

Easter Monday, I called the first lawyer. He told me it was probably nothing and not to worry about going alone. I called the other lawyer, Mr. Moore. He wasn't in, so I left a message. I tried to get a clergy friend of mine to go with me, but he wasn't available. It was after five now and the second lawyer had not called me back. The weeds began to choke me. I prayed for courage.

I went home and began to panic. The words ran through my head over and over again, "...We have to ask you to keep this confidential because we are conducting a very important investigation." "...We have to ask you to keep this confidential ..."

I asked God to go before me into the room and protect me from whatever this was. "You know that no one else can go with me," I said, "So I trust you to go with me. Just the two of us." I opened my Bible randomly and flipped some pages, looking for comfort. The pages fell open to a little read book for me, the book of Ruth. As I skimmed the page searching for something, ANYTHING, my eye caught several underlined verses in chapter 3. *"And now, my daughter, don't be afraid. I will do for you all you ask. All my fellow townsmen know that you are a woman of noble character"* (Ruth 3:11).

A warm sense of peace came over me and I rested for the next day.

Tuesday came and I was calmly resolved to going to the two o'clock meeting with only God. About 11a.m., the phone rang. It was Mr. Moore's secretary. She told me not go to the meting before I came to see him. I was half encouraged, but she seemed so tense I was half afraid again. I thanked God for the response and again asked Him to go with and protect me.

I found out that Mr. Moore was already representing others in the case and knew the players well. It was a drug trafficking case. After a few questions, he knew I wasn't involved. He called the postal inspector's office and told them that since there was no subpoena, I was not coming.

They had told him that the 'informal meeting' was actually a questioning session with a *federal* postal investigator, an FBI and a DEA agent. They wanted me to testify against a dealer in a grand jury hearing on Friday. I was a suspect because I met two criteria of other accomplices: I was black and female. I still felt trapped. If I didn't testify, the government could take my freedom. If I did, the dealers, whoever they were, could take my life. No one seemed to care about any of that.

My lawyer said the only answer was a handwriting analysis. I'd take it Thursday and the results should be back before the hearing. If the signature was mine, I'd testify; if not, I was free and clear. The tests confirmed the truth and my name was removed from the witness list *the day of the hearing*.

I had been snatched from the fire with not one minute of formal questioning, not one hour in court, and not one penny in lawyer's fees. My lawyer had refused to charge me, because he thought I was "good people." It was finally *over*. The next days were filled with rest and praise! Seven days had seemed like an eternity.

I look back over those days and realize that anything could have happened to me had I not consulted and trusted in God. My ignorance of my rights and trust in the fairness of the world would have let me attend that first meeting alone and unprotected. Instead, God had stepped in with His infinite wisdom and forced me to rely only on Him. He kept His promise and preserved my life and my reputation.

My experience has taught me that no situation is too dire or worldly, or complicated, or too far gone to be resolved by the Lord's mighty hand!

> *"He rescues and he saves; he performs signs and wonders in the heavens and on the earth."*
>
> *- Daniel 6:27*

The Next Time

Had it not been for a miracle in my life, I would not be alive today to witness other miracles and blessings in my life. The miracle began when I realized that no matter how much I prayed for its healing, the abusive marriage that I was in was not of God. "What therefore God hath joined together, let not man put asunder" (Mark 10:9), did not suit my case.

The Word of God says that Satan knows scripture; well he does. He used every one that he knew to keep me, a new convert, in fear. Each visit to the emergency room brought pleas from both the police and doctors for me to get out of my marriage before I became another statistic, my children orphans, and my husband one in the large number of black men behind prison walls. Being from the 'old school', I stayed, hoping things would change. But they didn't; the abuse continued and the fear remained.

I recall a dream that I had following an episode of violence. That night, my husband had taken the car keys from me in an attempt to keep me home. In the dream, God showed me that the same car would not start for my husband the next morning when he tried to leave for work. The next day, every red light in the car came on when he started it, exactly as I saw it in the dream. God was trying to tell me something - that He was on my side. "...lo, I am with you alway, even unto the end of the world" (Matthew 28:20). But I stayed, still afraid of how I would make it by myself with two young children.

One afternoon, I sat in the kitchen weeping over my situation, when the telephone rang. It was a niece of mine calling from Florida. She used to visit us in New York during her vacations from college but I had not talked to her in about five years. Why was she calling me 'out of the blue' and in prime time? When she asked why the tears, I shared with her what was going on in my life and how I feared leaving the situation. I know today that the call was from God. "It was you, Aunt Pam, that took care of the children when we lived in New York!" she said. Over and over she reminded me, "It was you Aunt Pam that worked, clothed and fed the children. It was you, Aunt Pam that made the home and was there for them." It was my 'wake up call'. I could take care of the children and myself. I always had.

Months passed and still nothing changed. It wasn't until I saw the fear in my children's eyes that I knew I had to do something; if not for my sake, then for theirs. The day I left home for the lawyer's office, I said to God, "I don't know what to do, but if you show me, I'll do it." I finally turned it over to him. God met me at the lawyer's office and stopped me when I started to procrastinate. When the lawyer asked what I wanted to do, I responded timidly, "Well, the next time he hits me..." Slamming his fist in the desk, he demanded, "Why wait for the next time?" It was another 'wake up call'. I signed the papers.

Today, I experience the greatest miracle of all, the miracle of LOVE. "For God so loved PAM that He gave his only begotten Son." I didn't become a statistic, but a strong child of God who is not ashamed to tell of his love wherever I go. My children are not orphans, but college graduates, young adults. My son is a parent himself and my daughter is a successful, productive worker in the field she has chosen. They both have committed their lives to Christ and are growing in faith daily. My children's father is not in that number of black men behind prison walls; he now pastors a local church! To God be the Glory! Great things he has done and He is worthy to be praised!!

"For he has rescued us from the dominion of darkness and brought us into the kingdom of the Son he loves, in whom we have redemption, the forgiveness of sins."

- Colossians 1:13-14

Deadly Choices

He was a friend of a good friend's whom I met in a club. He was very flashy and there was something about him that I liked. He always wore gold rings and thick gold chains and he always had money - always. He didn't seem to have a high paying job, but the dollars just flowed. Somehow it didn't faze me. The only time I ever saw him was at the club. He sometimes seemed to get jealous when other guys would talk to me or dance with me, but I didn't think he was honestly worried about what I was doing. Well, he was. There were all these huge warning signs, but I didn't want to see them.

Once he found out where I lived, he started just showing up to hang out. I knew it was dangerous, but I just enjoyed his company and I felt special that he was so kind and protective of me. People seemed to be very afraid of him, but he treated me like gold. Over the next few months, he got more and more possessive and I couldn't hide from the Reality that I was seeing a drug dealer who was very controlling and suspicious. The alarms finally started going off in my mind. "Get out of this!"

I had been raised in church and had wandered off a few years before. I was going to church sometimes but I wasn't living my faith and I didn't have a relationship with God. I had a magician God mentality. I would talk to him when I needed something. I was going to need Him soon.

One day during an argument, my friend suddenly turned on me and put a knife to my throat. He had never threatened me, so I couldn't tell if he was kidding or not. Well, it's true that God takes care of fools and babies, because out of ignorance or arrogance, I laid my head back, closed my eyes and said, "Go ahead, I'm going to a better place anyway!" He was shocked that I wasn't scared. But I was. By now, I was being followed and the fear was eating me up. He wasn't going to let me out of his sight or his life.

I kept praying. That Christmas God told me to give him a collection of scriptures in an updated English version. When he opened it, he just started crying. After that day, I didn't see or hear from him for two months.

When he did show up, he looked different somehow. He hugged me and told me he had started reading the book and for the first time understood what the verses meant. He had stopped dealing and had decided to go back to church. We talked about his salvation and he asked me if I had accepted Christ.

"All you have to do is decide to accept him," he said. "You've already got what I've got! Just accept it!!" That was the beginning of a *personal* relationship between Christ and I.

A few days later, I felt like a film had been pulled off my eyes. Everything was brighter, more colorful and I felt so free! People told me I was glowing. I had a lot of reasons to do so. God had given me the most perfect way out of the mess I had created. He had given my friend a new and honorable life. It's funny, the same man who had threatened to take my life, was the one who led me to true Life. The Lord works in mysterious ways.

"The LORD will keep you from all harm— he will watch over your life; the LORD will watch over your coming and going both now and forevermore."

- Psalm 121:7-8

Answered Prayer

Miracle - An event that appears unexplainable by the laws of nature and so is held to be supernatural in origin or an act of God.

I struggled with the above definition of a miracle. I could not get past the words unexplainable, or supernatural. Unexplainable or supernatural in nature was not how I viewed miracles. My miracle was neither; it was God interceding on my behalf. Psalms 121 reassures me of this. "The LORD watches over you— the LORD is your shade at your right hand; the sun will not harm you by day, nor the moon by night" (Psalm 121:5-6).

A sister in Christ helped me with my struggle. Her definition of a miracle was 'answered prayer.' At that moment, the miracles of my life were before me. They were there all the time, just like God.

If not for answered prayer, I would not be here today. Time after time God was there, protecting me, leading, guiding, assuring and comforting. There have been many answered prayers in my life. The time a security guard standing less than three feet from me was shot in the leg; the time I fell asleep at the wheel traveling 55 mph and woke up as my car crossed over into a lane of oncoming traffic; when I stop breathing a hundred plus times a night due to sleep apnea, and God gently shakes me and reminds me to breathe. As miraculous as these events are, the one that stands out in my mind occurred before any of these.

During the summer months of my youth, I attended Day Camp and went on many field trips. One of the many trips that I particularly enjoyed was going to the beach. I loved water; mainly the salt water spray of the ocean against my face and the heavy waves against my body. The bigger the wave, the better. I loved riding the waves.

One day another camper and I were playing in the ocean. "Let's go out further, so we can catch the big ones," I said to my friend. So we did. Suddenly, a big wave came in and the ground beneath my feet was gone. My friend started to head back in. I remember calling out "Help me!" He turned back and extended his hand to me. Instead of allowing him to help me, I pulled him out in my anxiety, and now he was in the same predicament as I.

I tried to get back to shore, struggling to keep my head above water. At that moment, I remember looking toward the shore and seeing lifeguards running toward the water. The next thing I remember was a strong arm taking me under as a wave broke, then hearing someone telling me to relax and not to fight. I must have lost consciousness because when I opened my eyes I was on the beach, coughing and spitting up water. But I was alive. 'Answered Prayer.'

The next week as I passed the beach I saw this sign posted:

Swim at Your Own Risk
Lifeguards on Strike